C000186538

THE BROONS

Speak Broons with Confidence

THE BROONS

Speak Broons with Confidence

BLACK & WHITE PUBLISHING

First published 2018
by Black & White Publishing Ltd
Nautical House, 104 Commercial Street,
Edinburgh, EH6 6NF

1 3 5 7 9 10 8 6 4 2   18 19 20 21

ISBN: 978 1 910230 56 5

The Broons ®© DC Thomson & Co. Ltd 2018
Text by Euan Kerr

A CIP catalogue record for this book is available from
the British Library.

Typeset by Creative Link, Haddington
Printed and bound by Opolgraf, Poland

Introduction

Are you ever **'black affronted'** – highly
embarrassed – at not understanding all the Scottish
phrases and sayings uttered by The Broons? **'Dinna
Fash yersel'** – don't get over concerned – here's
your guide to how to speak just like Scotland's
Favourite Family.

In this domestic scene, Maw offers the two senior gentlemen of the family a **'mealie pudden'** – a sort of large oatmeal sausage. Her husband retorts that he would prefer **'stovies'** – a Scottish delicacy containing potatoes, meat and dripping. He insists that the dish should also contain real onions **'ingans'** and his father enthusiastically concurs.

The family admire a large, carved sideboard which
they believe is a present from Grandfather Brown.
They describe it as **'bonnie'** or beautiful, though
it is **'ower big for wis!'** – over large for us!
They wish to return it but there is a concern that
'Gran'paw wid be awfy pitten aboot!'
– the old fellow would be extremely upset at the slight.

Mr Brown and an old school acquaintance discuss
bygone times over a convivial pint. Paw becomes
nostalgic and would like to revisit old times just once
– **'juist wance'**. He recalls fishing with strings
and pins **'wi' strings an' preens'** and agrees
to meet up the following day – **'the morn'**.

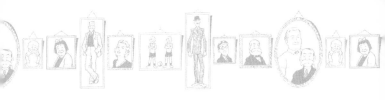

Paw is astounded and exclaims **'Jings!
Crivvens!! Michty me!!!'** Loosely translated
as Gosh! Cripes!! My goodness!!! The reason for his
discomfiture is that there has been a feline raid on his
smoked herring or **'kippers'**.

A workman generously offers some of the Browns a lift home with their bikes on the back of his lorry. Mrs Brown voices her appreciation – **'Jings! I'm glad o' this!'** Paw concurs saying **'Aw, thanks, Jock. The wife an' the weans are fair faggit!'** In other words, 'Thank you, John. My good lady and our young offspring are somewhat over exerted.'

Mrs Brown's father-in-law complains about the deficiency of the tea on offer – just a single sardine on toast. In response, Maw replies **'Weel, hoo did ye no' let me ken ye wis comin?'** Well why did you not inform me that you were dropping by? She goes on to say that she was eager to go on a shopping trip – **'I'm in a hurry to get doon the road!'**

Mr Brown and his father are transporting a door down a thoroughfare. A jocular gentleman calls out **'Hoi! Hae ye forgotten whaur ye bide?'** In other words, jokingly asking if the pair have had a memory lapse about where they dwell.

'A pot o' kail' which Grandfather Brown intends making, is otherwise known as a pot of soup. Although 'kail' is another word for cabbage it can also be used in general terms to describe mixed vegetable broth.

As the senior gentlemen of the Brown family collide with an unfortunate fellow, knocking him into an old-fashioned gramophone, Grandfather Brown utters the words **'Hey! Hoo can ye no' look whaur ye're gaun?'** He is asking the gent why he isn't more careful about where he is going, though it must be said that he is not entirely blameless.

The twins ask their brother, Horace, for an old rag
which they plan to fashion into a cloth football –
**'Gie's that auld rag. We want tae
mak' a clooty ba'!'**

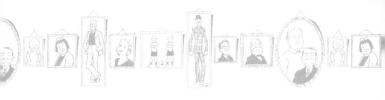

The twins have skewered their grandfather's headgear and plunged it to the bottom of a small pool. The old gentleman exclaims **'Ach! Ma bonnet's gone doon. Whaur is it!'** He is asking the whereabouts of his submerged headgear. Mrs Brown blames **'thae bairns'** – these children. The twins tell them not to worry, as they will retrieve the cloth item – **'Dinna fash yersel's – we'll pull it oot!'**

The twins are bored. One suggests that they construct a very small canvas dwelling – **'Whit aboot makin' juist a wee, wee tentie?'** Their young sister, though unable to read, imagines that the newspaper says that she is attractive and also rather cunning – **'Me is very bonny an' also Fly!'**

Mr Brown has had an unfortunate accident involving a newly varnished floor. He exclaims – **'Jings! Fegs! Michty me! There's ma breeks awa' next!** In other words – By jingo! Faith! My goodness! My trousers seem to have departed now.

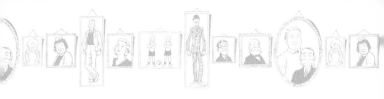

An overly enthusiastic door-to-door salesman has incurred Mrs Brown's wrath. She deals with him violently and sends him on his way telling him to depart forthwith! – **'Now get crackin'!'**

The two senior gentlemen of the Brown family are looking forward to a quiet board game – **'We'll get doon tae wir game o' ludo again.'** Upon hearing a knock on the door they suspect it may be **'mair guisers'** – more trick-or-treaters. Having been interrupted previously, they resolve not to answer – **'Weel, I'm no' gaun tae the door!'**

To please her husband, Mrs Brown has brought out her best china tea-set. She thinks she is being foolish – **'I ken I'm no' wise!'** She goes on to warn him to take extreme care – **'Be gey careful!'**

Mr Brown is most concerned that his middle son, Horace, has stayed out rather late. He castigates him **'Ye young deil's buckie! Ye wild scoot!'** – You imp of Satan! You reckless rascal! … He's not pleased!

As the family take afternoon tea, Mr Brown has to remonstrate with his twin sons – **'Now look whit ye've done – ye've skelt yer tea!'** See what has happened – you have overturned your hot beverage!

During a discussion about visiting a well-to-do lady, Mrs Brown berates her father-in-law saying **'We want tae keep wir end up, she's that tony and perjink'** – We do not wish to be humiliated, she's so neat and tidy.

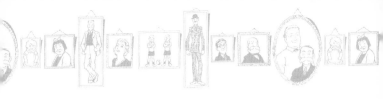

Grandfather again embarrasses the family by showing
his coarser side. Mrs Brown is highly humiliated
'I'm black affronted!' Her friend ponders
that **'Their gran'pa is still orra!'** – Their
grandfather is still dirty and uncouth!

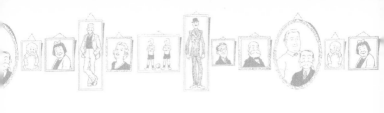

The Browns encounter a worried-looking lady. She confirms her concerns by saying **'Whit a bother I'm in.'** The reason for her disquietude is explained when she tells them **'Ma lum needs sweepin' an' I canna get a sweep.'** In other words, her chimney requires to be swept and she cannot find a chimney sweep to employ.

Horace presents his youngest sibling with a child's savings bank made of crockery – **'Here's a bankie for ye – a pirlie pig.'** The old Scots word 'pyrl' means to thrust or push into.

When Grandfather Brown claims that escapology is easy and he can do such tricks himself, one of his young grandsons says **'OF course! You can dae a'thing, ye auld Footer!'** – Of course you can do everything, you are someone who roams from one aimless task to another.

Mr Brown has sat on a newly varnished chair and is stuck fast. His son, Henry, describes him as a **'Daft auld gowk!'** – an awkward or foolish person. April Fool's Day can also be called Gowk Day in parts of Scotland.

Knowing that Mr Brown and his father are hiding in large earthenware jars to avoid housework, the ladies pour water into them, ostensibly to clean out the jars. The elderly pair emerge from their hiding places exclaiming, **'Help! I'm drookit!'** and **'I'm a' weet!'** In other words, they are both soaked to the skin (and serves them right!).

The two elderly Mr Browns have had similar accidents caused by jumping to catch a stray football. **'Oh, Jings! I've bust ma gallusses!'** says Mr Brown Jnr. – My goodness! My braces have snapped! His father says the same may have happened to him and adds **'I ken ma breeks are fa'in' doon!'** He knows that his trousers are in danger of dropping to the ground.

Mr Brown has agreed to take out a neighbour's infant – **'O.K., then, Maw. I'll tak' the wean.'** Mrs Brown reminds him **'An' dinna you Forget tae collect a' the messages I ordered!'** She is advising him not to overlook the groceries she has ordered.

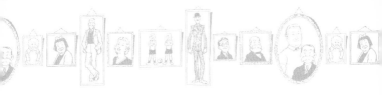

'Oh, crivvens! I've kicked it ower the dyke!' says Mr Brown, meaning he's just launched a football over a wall. His youngest daughter adds that he has smashed a lady's glass-pane – 'Ye've broke the wifie's windae!'

The Browns have been invited to a wedding but have
to make their way up an uneven roadway to get there.
Daphne is unhappy and expostulates **'Fancy haein'
tae walk through dubs tae a wedding!'**
She is surprised that they have to make their way
through puddles to such a prestigious occasion.

Whilst partaking in a leisurely game of putting, Daphne points out a nearby gentleman – **'That's a rare lookin' lad ower there Maggie.'** That's a fine-looking young gentleman over yonder, Margaret.

Mr Brown has received a **'jeelly nose'** from a
spring-loaded bureau drawer. This is a painful blow to
the nose which has caused some blood flow. A jeelly
nose can also be the result of fisticuffs.

The Brown parents are having trouble with a clock which does not keep accurate time. Mr Brown complains **'Ach, it's a scunner never kennin' the richt time.'** He is saying that it is a real nuisance that they are unable to ascertain the correct time of day.

THAT NIGHT YAWN~ JINGS! I'M TIRED! WHIT TIME IS IT ~ HALF-PAST TWELVE? OH, NO. IT'S ONLY TWELVE ~ THE CLOCK'S HALF AN HOUR FAST. IT'S HIGH TIME HEN AN' JOE AN' MAGGIE AN' DAPHNE GOT HAME.

ACH, IT'S A SCUNNER NEVER KENNIN' THE RICHT TIME. I'LL PIT THE CLOCK BACK TAE MIDNIGHT. NOW WE'LL KEN WHIT'S WHIT!

As the men of the family labour over the removal of a tree root, Mr Brown remarks that **'It's a gey tough job.'** This means that it is a task of some considerable difficulty.

As the family harangue Henry on various topics, he ripostes **'Ach! Awa' an' chase yersel's!'** He is telling them, in no uncertain terms, to jolly well buzz off!

Grandfather is staying in the family home. He is to sleep in a makeshift bed up on the clothes pulley. He causes some disturbance to his family which results in Mr Brown saying, **'Juist bide up there oot o' the road.'** He is simply requesting that his father stay in his aerial sleeping place. He concludes by intimating that the senior gentleman is an old pest – **'auld scunner!'**

Mr Brown refers to his weather forecasting gadget to see if he requires extra clothing as he is going out. **'I'm awa' oot.'** He decides this would be wise as **'The wee mannie's come oot o' his door.'** – In other words the small gentleman has exited his apartment. Henry and Joseph scoff at this saying **'That's a lot o' blethers.'** They believe that their father is talking utter nonsense.

The male siblings have been hiking and exhaustedly tell their father and grandfather **'We're fair' wabbit!'** – We are exceedingly tired and exhausted. Alternatively, in their vernacular, they could have said they were **'fair' puggled.'**

The men have used a book Mrs Brown has bought them to fix an uneven table making it **'shoogly'** or rather wobbly. Did they fix it?

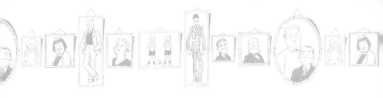

Out in the country, two young fellows ask Grandfather
Brown where the Browns' dwelling is as they wish to go
shooting and fishing. The old chap informs them **'The
shootin' is ower at the midden.'** – The
shooting is over by the refuse tip. He goes on to tell
them that the fishing is at the **'burn'** or stream.

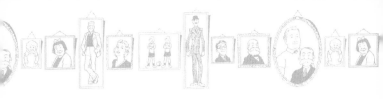

Mr Brown is irate about people constantly borrowing from them. He refuses to loan a cake stand and tells his sons **'That's the way tae tell them whaur tae get aff!'** – That's the way to tell them to go away immediately!

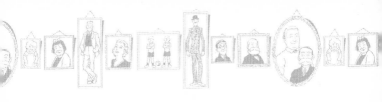

Mrs Brown cautions her husband to take care as he is rather elderly to be attempting a difficult climb. Mr Brown retorts 'Ach! Dinna be daft! I'm no' feart tae climb a greenie pole!' In other words, he is telling his wife to hush her foolish talk as he is not scared of ascending a clothes pole.

Mr Brown discusses the faults of a family named Duncan. **'Their auldest laddie's humphy-backit, cross-eyed an' impident.'** – Their oldest boy is rather round-shouldered, has a lazy eye condition and is prone to insolence. He then describes young Miss Duncan as **'A thin dreep like the Faither.'** – A tall, undernourished person like her male parent.

~AN' THEIR AULDEST LADDIE'S HUMPHY-BACKIT, CROSS-EYED AN' IMPIDENT. THE LASSIE'S A THIN DREEP LIKE THE FAITHER, AN' SHE HAS KNOCK-KNEES AN' FLAT FEET. AN' THE WEE LAD'S GROWIN' UP TAE BE AS UGLY AS HIS MITHER. "D"~ IT'S THE DUNCANS!! BUT WHAUR DOES THE SURPRISE COME IN?

THOUGHT:~ JINGS! PAW'S RICHT ENOUGH!

SSH~SH

Mr and Mrs Brown overhear two neighbours having words. One counters the other one's jibes by dismissively stating **'Awa' an' bile yer heid, ye haverin' besom.'** – Go and immerse your head in boiling water, you nonsensical troublemaker.

'Thae Broons think they're awfy smairt, but they're a bunch o' nyaffs – fae the wee drochle o' a Faither tae thon claespeg, Hen. Him that thinks that he's the real Airchie wi' his bowler hat an' his padded shouthers.' – These Browns consider themselves of superior intellect while in fact they are a collection of insignificant people – from that puny little runt of a father to that tall, thin Henry. He believes himself to be the top dog with his posh headgear and shoulder pads.

After an unfortunate incident involving a muddy
bog, the ladies of the family comment that the
Brown gentlemen **'Look awfy sichts wi'
the mud richt up yer breeks.'** They are
passing comment that the gents are a dreadful sight
with mud to the top of their legwear.

Margaret and Henry are irked by the dreadful cacophony their younger brothers and sister are making. Henry suggests **'Awa' ben the hoose an' play some other game!"** – He wishes them to take themselves off to another part of the home where they might consider other pastimes.

As the family travel by train to the Firth of Forth, Mr Brown remarks that he would have preferred going for a trip down the River Clyde – **'I'd raither hae had a trip doon the water.'**

THIS IS A' GRAN'PAW'S IDEA! FANCY US GOIN' TAE THE FIRTH OF FORTH FOR THE WEEK-END. I'D RAITHER HAE HAD A TRIP DOON THE WATER.

OH! BUT THIS IS A RARE CHANGE— AN' WE'RE GETTIN' THE USE O' AUNTIE JEANNIE'S COTTAGE WHILE SHE'S AWA' THE WEEK-END!

AN' I'M GOIN' FISHIN'. I'VE GOT MA GEAR A' READY IN THIS PARCEL. A' I NEED IS A FEW LANG POLES

HUH! YE'LL NO' CATCH ONYTHING.

Mr Brown's elder sons are about to play a practical joke on their poor father. He comments that he **'mind seein' this trick done years syne but I canna mind whit happens!'** – He remembers seeing the trick performed many years ago but he has no recollection of the outcome.

Mr Brown has 'accidentally' caused several rotten eggs to rain down on an unwelcome guest. He apologetically offers to wipe away some of the mess with an old cloth scrap – **'I'll dicht ye up wi' this auld rag!'**

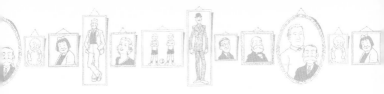

The youngest of the Brown family has exchanged a gentleman's pipe for one of her own designed to blow bubbles. The gent reacts unfavourably to inhaling the soapy liquid – The word **'FEECH!'** is used to describe his distaste. He also states that he's **'Gonna be seeck!'** – He expects to regurgitate.

As one twin comments that a fellow named **'Airchy Ramsay'** – Archibald Ramsay – does not believe that Mr Brown is proficient at bowls, the other twin states that Archibald's father is only capable of playing a low-stakes card game – **'Ha'penny nap!'**

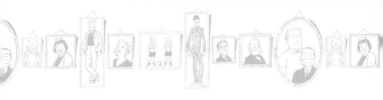

The family are enjoying an evening at the cinema. They are making something of a disturbance so Mrs Brown comments **'Wheesht, Maggie! Ye'll get pit oot!'** – Be silent, Margaret, or you shall be ejected!

Mr Brown has had a mishap resulting in his trousers being shredded. He wishes to hide from approaching strangers and asks where he can go. His youngest daughter suggests **'Ahent this dike!'** – Behind this wall!

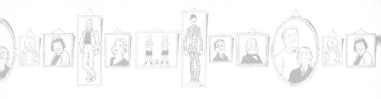

As Mr and Mrs Brown amble home, Mrs Brown comments that their daughter **'Maggie is bringin' her new click tae the hoose the nicht!'** In other words, Margaret is presenting her new romantic acquaintance at the Brown domicile that evening.

As Mr and Mrs Brown look in on a riotous party, Mrs B comments **'Oh, michty! Whit a rammy!'** My goodness! What a commotion! Mr Brown suggests that they just sit in the **'lobby'** or vestibule.

The older Brown gentlemen admire a photograph from bygone years when they went to the most expensive seats in the theatre. Son, Joseph, tells them **'That wis juist swank!'** – They were just showing off and pretending to be toffs.

Whilst speaking of an old friend, Grandfather Brown describes him as being 'awfy fly' – this does not mean he has wings and buzzes, rather it tells us that he is rather crafty and sneaky.

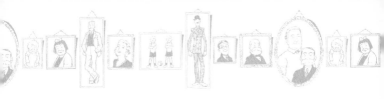

In this scene Mr Brown remarks that the table is **'fell near the door'** – rather near the door. Daphne comments that **'this is a gey hot cup o' tea!'** She means that it is more than a little hot.

In this Easter scene, Mr Brown enthuses that **'It's a braw day – we'll hae a rare time.'** – It's a glorious day and they are going to enjoy it greatly.

As a gent injures himself alighting from a tram, Mrs Brown describes him as a **'puir sowel!'** She means that he is an unfortunate fellow. A **'puir sowel'** can also mean someone who is ailing and hardly able to look after themselves.

Mr Brown is rudely awakened. He says **'Listen tae that clatter o' milk bottles!'** To clatter is to make a loud, cacophonous sound. You can also be **'clattered'** at football if you receive an over-robust tackle.

That's all folks –

now you can Speak Broons with Confidence!